A B C

Illustrated by Angela Mills

BRIMAX · NEWMARKET · ENGLAND

Aa

a is for **a**crobat

Is the acrobat wearing a hat?
What else can you find that starts with **a**?

Bb

b is for **b**icycle

Which bicycle is blue?
What else can you find that starts with **b**?

Cc

c is for **c**at

What time does the clock say?
What else can you find that starts with **c**?

Dd

d is for **d**olphin

Point to the dog in the picture.
What else can you find that starts with **d**?

Ee

e is for elephant

What is the elephant holding in his trunk?
What else can you find that starts with **e**?

Ff

f is for **f**air

Where is the merry-go-round?
What else can you find that starts with **f**?

Gg

g is for **g**loves

Who is wearing red gloves?
What else can you find that starts with **g**?

Hh

h is for **h**olly

Point to the holly in the picture.
What else can you find that starts with **h**?

Ii

i is for igloo

Who is eating ice-cream?
What else can you find that starts with **i**?

Jj

j is for **j**uggler

What is the juggler juggling with?
What else can you find that starts with **j**?

Kk

k is for **k**angaroo

Who is flying the kite?
What else can you find that starts with **k**?

Ll

l is for lake

How many boats are there on the lake?
What else can you find that starts with l?

Mm

m is for **m**ouse

Who is wearing mittens?
What else can you find that starts with **m**?

Nn

n is for **n**est

How many birds are in the nest?
What else can you find that starts with **n**?

Oo

o is for **o**wl

Can you see the owl?
What else can you find that starts with **o**?

Pp

p is for **p**icnic

How many plates are there?
What else can you find that starts with **p**?

Qq

q is for **q**ueen

Who is hiding under the quilt?
What else can you find that starts with **q**?

Rr

r is for **r**iver

Can you see the rainbow?
What else can you find that starts with **r**?

Ss

s is for **s**andcastle

How many sandcastles can you count?
What else can you find that starts with **s**?

Tt

t is for trumpet

Who is playing the trumpet?
What else can you find that starts with t?

Uu

u is for **u**mbrella

How many rabbits are under the umbrella?
What else can you find that starts with **u**?

Vv

v is for **v**iolin

How many flowers are in the vase?
What else can you find that starts with **v**?

Ww

w is for **w**ig-wam?

Who is hiding in the wig-wam?
What else can you find that starts with **w**?

Xx

x is for **x**ylophone?

Who is playing the xylophone?
What else can you find that starts with **x**?

Yy

y is for **y**acht

How many rabbits are on the yacht?
What else can you find that starts with **y**?

Zz

z is for **z**ebra

What is the zebra doing?
What else can you find that starts with **z**?